CONTENTS

KEY TERMS

The following definitions are provided for the purpose of clarifying this plan and should not be considered official definitions unless so noted.

Customer: Any entity or individual external to DSCA that relies on a security cooperation activity or process to achieve a specific output or a specific outcome (e.g. foreign partner, USG agency/MILDEP, industry).

Implementing Agency: The Military Department or defense agency responsible for executing military assistance programs. With respect to foreign military sales, the Military Department or defense agency assigned responsibility by the Defense Security Cooperation Agency to prepare a Letter of Offer and Acceptance (LOA) and to implement a foreign military sales (FMS) case. The implementing agency is responsible for the overall management of the actions that will result in delivery of the materials or services set forth in the LOA accepted by a foreign country or international organization.

Partner (also Partner Nation, International Partner): An international entity, most often a foreign defense and security establishment, that is the beneficiary of security cooperation programs and activities.

Security Assistance: A group of programs authorized by the Foreign Assistance Act of 1961, as amended, and the Arms Export Control Act of 1976, as amended, or other related statutes by which the United States provides defense articles, military training, and other defense-related services, by grant, loan, cash sale, or lease, in furtherance of national policies and objectives (JP 1-02, as amended through 14 April 2006).

Security Cooperation: The full continuum of activities undertaken by the Department of Defense to encourage and enable international partners to work with the United States to achieve strategic objectives. It encompasses all DoD interactions with foreign defense and security establishments, including all DoD-administered security assistance programs, that build defense and security relationships promoting specific U.S. security interests, including all international armaments cooperation activities and security assistance activities; that develop allied and friendly military capabilities for self-defense and multinational operations; and that provide U.S. forces with peacetime and contingency access to host nations (DoD Directive 5132.03).

> ▸ **Security Cooperation Community (SCC):** A subset of USG executive branch entities within the Security Cooperation enterprise directly responsible for managing or executing security cooperation programs or the policies that affect those programs.

> ▸ **Security Cooperation Enterprise (SCE):** The network of entities engaged in any element of security cooperation programs, either as providers or beneficiaries. This includes USG agencies, Congress, foreign partners, and industry.

> ▸ **Security Cooperation Workforce:** Employees of USG agencies within the Security Cooperation community.

MESSAGE FROM THE DIRECTOR

I have worked in the Security Cooperation community in various capacities for many years, and am continually impressed by the talent and commitment of our workforce. I have seen first-hand how the community meets the enormous challenges that emerge from dynamic policy decisions, a rapidly changing environment, and fluctuating resources. That is why I am so honored to present our strategy for the future, which we call DSCA Vision 2020. My expectation is that organizations across the community will align themselves to this plan, and that we will all hold ourselves accountable for achieving the goals set out in these pages.

DSCA Vision 2020 was built through a strenuous bottom-up process that drew participants from the directorates and entities under the DSCA umbrella. We vigorously sought input from stakeholders across the community, and I firmly believe our strategic plan is better because we did. My heartfelt thanks go to everyone who participated in our strategic planning process. Your contributions and continued support are critically important to our collective success.

As I took the helm at DSCA, I was confronted with just how complex our challenges are, and how complicated our work has become. The bottom-up planning process confirmed what I already believed to be true: DSCA has an amazing track record of excellence and has the right people to take the Agency to the next level. Let me be clear: It is because of the presence – not a lack – of talent and commitment in our workforce that DSCA Vision 2020 plans for an aggressive step into the future. This strategic plan is not about change for its own sake. It is about positioning DSCA to play an active role in advancing the community beyond the sum of its parts. The intention of this strategic plan is to leverage DSCA resources both to build on the community's strengths and address our weaknesses in order to better achieve U.S. national security and foreign policy objectives.

Despite the thorough and inclusive approach the DSCA team has taken in the strategic planning process, many vigorous debates remain before us. I welcome these difficult conversations as opportunities to learn and grow. As a community of professionals, we can move forward together. It is in this spirit that I am proud to publish DSCA Vision 2020.

MESSAGE FROM THE MANAGEMENT TEAM

As DSCA's management team, we are dedicated to achieving DSCA Vision 2020 by implementing the goals, objectives, and initiatives laid out in this document. We affirm our pledge to the Agency's values and to holding each other to the same high standards to which we hold the broader workforce. DSCA Vision 2020 outlines the appropriate course of action for addressing the challenges of the coming decade. Together, as a community, we will take a bold step into the future!

Deputy Director

Principal Director for Business Operations

Principal Director for Administration & Management

Principal Director for Building Partner Capacity

Principal Director for Information Technology/Chief Information Officer

Principal Director for Strategy

Principal Director for Security Assistance

Chief Performance Officer

Principal Director for Legislative Management

General Counsel

EXECUTIVE SUMMARY

Since its establishment, the Defense Security Cooperation Agency (DSCA) has been directing, administering, and providing DoD-wide guidance for the execution of programs for which it is responsible. This role is made difficult by the rapidly changing international environment, by resource scarcity, and by the overall complexity of the Security Cooperation community (SCC). It requires a whole-of-government approach to building capacities with our partners that support U.S. interests. DSCA Vision 2020 lays out a plan for DSCA to enable such an approach by the Security Cooperation enterprise (SCE), focusing on three interlocking areas: (1) synchronizing security cooperation activities, (2) meeting customer expectations, and (3) ensuring the effective and efficient use of community resources.

DSCA will work with all stakeholders to **calibrate its roles and responsibilities** in order to address ambiguity, eliminate redundancies across the community, and ensure the appropriate delegation of responsibility for its programs. DSCA will also establish a strategy to effectively **manage human capital** within the Agency and across the community to ensure that the right people fill the right positions and have the necessary resources to execute their duties. DSCA will lead the community in supporting the workforce with **enhanced knowledge management,** including a more effective information technology architecture and a culture of organizational learning.

This foundation will enable the synchronization of security cooperation efforts to meet customer expectations – whether in **aligning efforts to strategic priorities** issued by the White House, Department of Defense, or relevant interagency organizations; **enabling more responsive industry participation in security cooperation;** or responding to international partner requirements to **remain a provider of choice.**

To synchronize the community and meet customer expectations, we must use our resources effectively and efficiently. DSCA therefore will use its authorities and resources to **incentivize community performance, innovation, and responsiveness**. DSCA will aggressively **optimize the management and execution of DSCA programs** through robust assessment efforts and continuous process improvement projects.

DSCA will use a strategy-to-task approach to address these areas of focus and hold itself accountable for this strategic plan. DSCA will develop annual implementation plans to ensure that DSCA Vision 2020 goals, objectives, and initiatives are achieved. The implementation plans will assign specific time-bound tasks to DSCA action officers, and progress will be regularly monitored at the highest levels of DSCA leadership.

DSCA Vision 2020 is a strategy for fulfilling our vision: **Enable a whole-of-government effort to build and maintain networks of defense relationships that achieve U.S. national security goals.** By focusing on synchronization, customer expectations, and effectiveness and efficiency, DSCA will continue to play a central role in the Security Cooperation community well into the future.

OUR ENVIRONMENT AND APPROACH

U.S. national security and foreign policy interests can be achieved only by working closely with and building the capacities and capabilities of our partners. As the 2014 Quadrennial Defense Review states, "we will continue to operate in close concert with our allies and partners... because no country alone can address the globalized challenges we collectively face." Confronting those challenges requires the Security Cooperation community (SCC) to perform at the highest possible level. However, several factors hamper our efforts.

▸ Competition for resources is high and the United States' reliance on its partners increases in environments of fiscal austerity.

▸ It is difficult to align efforts and develop corporate knowledge across the Security Cooperation enterprise (SCE). The legal and regulatory environment is complex, and most U.S. Government agencies within the SCE are not exclusively focused on security cooperation functions. They therefore have diverse business cultures, operating procedures, authorities, and understandings of strategic guidance.

▸ The nature of international relationships is rapidly changing and we face a more diverse, capable, and competitive international environment. With a broader field of competitors comes a wider spectrum of areas in which the United States must compete. The increased connectivity of the global economy and information infrastructure vastly accelerates the speed at which relationships are formed, maintained, and complicated. Simply planning as a community is insufficient. This emerging environment favors those who can pursue their national interests by adapting to unforeseen challenges and opportunities.

In order to establish and maintain the relationships so vital to our strategic interests, the United States must be proactive in meeting the unique and dynamic needs of our partners. In order to compete, the SCC must be able to identify and process these needs and pull together various programs and services into a customized solution compatible with U.S. national interests and law, and is able to compete successfully in the current environment. Such convergence requires a more unified whole-of-government approach – an approach that is already mandated for the programs covered by Presidential Policy Directive 23 on Security Sector Assistance.

DSCA strives to lead the Security Cooperation community in the following areas:

Synchronizing Security Cooperation Activities

▸ Working closely with the Office of the Deputy Assistant Secretary of Defense for Security Cooperation, DSCA will lead the community in better coordinating the delegation and sequencing of efforts, and in collaborating across the SCE. Its role includes facilitating decision-making that addresses gaps, redundancies, and conflicts, and that achieves long-term objectives. It also entails building adaptability into our processes so the enterprise can anticipate and respond to emergent and dynamic requirements.

Meeting Customer Expectations

▸ There is a customer in everything DSCA does, whether it is another U.S. Government organization, industry, or an international partner. The complexity of modern challenges requires solutions that are tailored and artfully deployed. Properly identifying and executing to customer expectations enables the U.S. Government to find more complete solutions to its challenges while remaining competitive in the global marketplace.

Ensuring Effectiveness and Efficiency

▸ Effectiveness and efficiency are goals in everything we do. DSCA must be able to draw on all its security cooperation tools to find the best solution for a given task – and it must do so while constrained by declining resources. DSCA will lead the community in the sustainable use of resources through business process improvement, modernization, and coordinated assessments of community effectiveness and efficiency.

FUNDAMENTALS

Mission

▸ Lead the Security Cooperation community (SCC) in developing and executing innovative security cooperation solutions that support mutual U.S. and partner interests.

Vision

▸ Enable a whole-of-government effort to build and maintain networks of relationships that achieve U.S. national security goals.

Values

▸ **Leadership:** We are a U.S. Government-wide source for security cooperation solutions. We expect our organization and our workforce to lead the community toward accomplishing national, regional, and country objectives.

▸ **Integrity:** We adhere to the highest ethical and professional standards. In order to build partnerships based on trust, integrity must be at the core of all we do.

▸ **Teamwork:** We are committed to the Security Cooperation enterprise (SCE) as a whole-of-government effort. We understand the importance of working together to build and sustain enduring relationships with our international partners.

▸ **Innovation:** We strive for organizational creativity and adaptability. These characteristics are essential to our success in today's evolving strategic environment.

▸ **Efficiency:** We are trusted stewards of U.S. taxpayer and partner nation funds. We strive to achieve our mission in the most efficient way possible while maintaining our commitment to effectiveness and quality.

LAYING THE FOUNDATION

1. Calibrating DSCA's Roles and Responsibilities

Goal: Ensure that DSCA's official roles and responsibilities support DSCA Vision 2020.

End State: Official issuances clearly codify the level of DSCA responsibility necessary for the efficient and effective execution of DSCA-managed security cooperation programs and initiatives.

Objective 1.1: Lead the Security Cooperation community in clarifying and codifying Agency roles and responsibilities in order to eliminate ambiguity and redundancy and better align with strategic guidance and existing directives.

Initiative	Dates
a. Conduct an internal review of existing DoD and SCC directives and recommend necessary amendments to eliminate ambiguities, inefficiencies, misalignments, and gaps that inhibit the effective and efficient execution of DSCA-managed programs.	Oct 2014 – Sept 2016
b. Contribute to the updating of all forms of guidance and security cooperation processes required to ensure that DSCA equities are represented in accordance with the Agency's mission.	Oct 2014 – Sept 2016
c. Engage security cooperation stakeholders to clarify roles and responsibilities related to program oversight, management, and the general execution of security cooperation activities.	Apr 2015 – Sept 2016
d. Review and update, as required, program-specific information papers, execution guidance, and training materials.	Oct 2015 – Sept 2017

Objective 1.2: Initiate and participate in a thorough review of the security cooperation workforce that calibrates the roles and responsibilities of job categories to simplify business processes and eliminate unnecessary redundancy.

Initiative	Dates
a. Lead a community-wide inventory of core security cooperation positions and recommend amendments to roles and responsibilities necessary to eliminate ambiguities, inefficiencies, misalignments, and gaps.	Oct 2014 – Sept 2016
b. Review and update, as required, position descriptions, program-specific information papers, execution guidance, and training materials to reflect new roles and responsibilities.	June 2016 – Sept 2018

2. Managing Human Capital Across the Community

Goal: Effectively manage DSCA human capital and the Security Cooperation community.

End State: A talented and motivated security cooperation workforce efficiently resourced to achieve success while meeting the challenges of today and anticipating the challenges of tomorrow.

The following objectives and their associated initiatives and metrics are presented in more detail in DSCA's Human Capital Strategy.

Objective 2.1: Establish and maintain a community workforce structure sized to meet workload requirements and to advance our Agency's strategic mission and role in security cooperation.

Objective 2.2: Optimize community recruitment, hiring, assignment, and retention of our people to support mission requirements and avoid gaps in mission-critical knowledge, skills, and competencies.

Objective 2.3: Ensure that workforce possession and continuity of critical skills, knowledge, and leadership, and provide opportunities for community-wide development through succession planning, training, and workforce development programs.

Objective 2.4: Maximize results-oriented leadership and employee performance in direct support of the security cooperation mission.

Objective 2.5: Ensure human capital and community management practices are equitable, accountable, transparent, and in compliance with the law.

3. Enhancing Knowledge Management

Goal: Establish and implement community-wide standards for knowledge management.

End State: Security Cooperation community data systems and information sharing practices provide a near real-time view of community activities, facilitate organizational learning, and enable strategic decision making, including on future activities and resource allocation.

For our purposes, knowledge management is the use of information technology, business processes, and organizational design to facilitate the collection, storage, and integration of information and distributed knowledge across a network so that the nodes of the network can simultaneously contribute to and benefit from a common operating picture that informs decision making.

Objective 3.1: Optimize current and emerging data systems and information sharing to facilitate efficient business processes, satisfy customer requirements, and enable strategic thinking across the spectrum of security cooperation activities.

Initiative	Dates
a. Eliminate redundancy in data systems and ensure that systems include adequate functionality for current and future business processes.	Oct 2014 – Sept 2020
b. Implement a detailed plan for DSCA's migration to the Global Theater Security Cooperation Management Information System (G-TSCMIS) and for DSCA to help the community effectively use of G-TSCMIS as the authoritative data system of the SCC.	Oct 2014 – Sept 2020
c. Improve situational awareness and the ability to meet various reporting requirements by reviewing the Military Articles & Service List (MASL) construct and viable alternatives.	Oct 2016 – Sept 2017

Objective 3.2: Establish standard methodologies and instill a culture of organizational learning that systematizes the collection, analysis, and distribution of suggested approaches to recurring activities.

Initiative	Dates
a. Facilitate the systematic documentation and sharing of community insights related to the performance of recurring activities, and develop suggested approaches that inform planning, improve processes, and enhance employee training.	Oct 2014 - Dec 2015

SYNCHRONIZING TO MEET CUSTOMER EXPECTATIONS

4. Aligning Activities and Resource Allocation to Broader Strategic Priorities

Goal: Prioritize the achievement of U.S. Government strategic goals in executing DSCA-managed activities, programs, and resource allocation.

End State: DSCA leads the Security Cooperation community in synchronizing the resourcing, management, and execution of its programs in order to effectively prioritize the achievement of specified strategic outcomes.

Objective 4.1: Improve internal DSCA information sharing, communication, and synchronization of efforts to enable employees to think strategically across the spectrum of security cooperation activities.

Initiative	Dates
a. Transition DSCA to a "matrixed organization" and establish Integrated Regional Teams that prioritize and synchronize DSCA-managed activities while balancing USG objectives with partner nation expectations.	Oct 2014 – Dec 2014
b. Use a DSCA-wide engagement calendar tracking significant events, milestones, and recurring activities to improve the timeliness and quality of planning processes and products.	Oct 2014 – Sept 2015
c. Modernize DSCA's infrastructure to facilitate increased communication and synchronization across functions, and to enable a mobile workforce with a reduced physical footprint.	Oct 2014 – Sept 2016

Objective 4.2: Inform resource allocation and the planning and execution of DSCA-managed programs by structured analysis that derives priorities from national, regional, and DoD strategic guidance.

Initiative	Dates
a. Develop and use mechanisms to understand, address, and support the strategic priorities and concerns of security cooperation stakeholder.	Oct 2014 – Mar 2016
b. Manage long- and short-term bilateral engagement strategies that inform the use of DSCA resources so that DSCA activities better align with USG strategic guidance.	Oct 2014 – Mar 2016
c. Use regional roadmaps to advance the achievement of desired 5- to 10-year security cooperation end states, and to identify DSCA's ability to mitigate the effects of likely resource constraints and security challenges.	Oct 2014 – Sept 2016

Objective 4.3: Facilitate interagency collaboration with and external understanding of the Security Cooperation community to improve DSCA involvement in intra-agency Phase 0 planning and enable synchronization among security cooperation programs.

Initiative	Dates
a. Develop strategies for improving stakeholder understanding of DSCA's tools and for positioning DSCA to better support security cooperation-related activities.	Oct 2014 – Mar 2016

b. Coordinate with stakeholders and identify plans, objectives, and milestones to conduct recurring regional program reviews in order to synchronize activities, create synergy in response to USG initiatives, and develop security cooperation solutions.	Oct 2014 – Sept 2016
c. Participates in interagency strategic planning processes and proactively provide guidance on building policy options that consider the feasibility of execution.	Oct 2014 – Sept 2020

5. Enabling More Responsive Industry Participation in Security Cooperation

Goal: Sustain a whole-of-government effort to facilitate more responsive industry participation in security cooperation.

End State: The Security Cooperation community partners with industry to actively apply innovative approaches to fulfilling international capability requirements.

Objective 5.1: Conduct structured analyses that inform U.S. Government decision making on supporting industry's participation in security cooperation efforts.

Initiative	Dates
a. Annually publish increasingly accurate FMS Forecasts and Javits Reports that project FMS activities and support effective planning and budgeting for security cooperation.	Oct 2014 - Sept 2020
b. Develop technology roadmaps that compare key aspects of the export readiness of U.S. systems or technology solutions to partners' capability requirements in order to support forecasted competitions.	Oct 2014 – Sept 2020
c. Implement, where appropriate, a strategic framework that supports USG efforts to help define partner requests.	Oct 2014 – Sept 2020
d. Identify and promote technology release decisions that support security cooperation priorities.	Oct 2014 – Sept 2020

Objective 5.2: Facilitate industry engagements that provide and capitalize on security cooperation opportunities.

Initiative	Dates
a. Lead DoD support to tradeshows to ensure that security cooperation objectives are appropriately prioritized.	Oct 2014 – Sept 2020
b. Implement a methodology for planning industry engagements that help achieve technology roadmaps.	Oct 2014 – Sept 2020
c. Promote a DoD methodology to implement approved advocacy plans.	Oct 2014 – Sept 2016

6. Remaining a Provider of Choice for Our International Customers

Goal: Use the Foreign Military Sales (FMS) process and supporting activities to facilitate the building and maintenance of international relationships by meeting customer expectations and making FMS competitive in a diverse international environment.

End State: Prospective international customers view the United States as a provider of choice because of positive and repeatable experiences with the FMS process.

Objective 6.1: Optimize the use of customer funds across the community.

Initiative	Dates
a. Encourage transparency by identifying the specific officials within the United States and a partner nation who have authority to make commitments on their country's behalf.	Oct 2014 – Dec 2015
b. Assess "standard level of service" implementation and evaluate potential alternatives.	Oct 2014 – Aug 2016
c. Evaluate the use of a tiered administrative surcharge and examine other potential alternatives.	Oct 2014 – Aug 2016
d. Conduct a major review of each surcharge and evaluate assessment and collection methodologies.	Oct 2014 – Sept 2017
e. Review processes that use FMS customer funds – including Stand-By Letter of Credit Program, termination liability, case closure, payment schedules, and training pricing – to eliminate inefficiencies and the unnecessary retention of customer funds.	Oct 2017 – Sept 2018

Objective 6.2: Adapt the FMS process to changing business practices and purchaser requirements with innovative business models and more accommodating business rules.

Initiative	Dates
a. Propose legislative changes to permit FMS purchasers to allow U.S. contractors specified in a valid commercial export authorization to have temporary possession of or access to defense articles procured via FMS without a separate retransfer authorization in order to perform integration, repair, refurbishment, or upgrade.	Oct 2014- 2015 Legislative Cycle
b. Develop strategies to support defense equipment/training sharing initiatives.	Oct 2014 – Sept 2016
c. Reform the management of Supply Discrepancy Reports to improve responsiveness to the customer while making the review process less labor-intensive for USG implementing agencies.	Oct 2014 – Sept 2015
d. Explore and develop options for using LOA service lines to support leases of defense articles.	Oct 2015 – Mar 2016

Objective 6.3: Increase confidence in FMS as a procurement option for partner nations by providing greater and more structured customer visibility and participation during the Pre-LOR (Letter of Request) and case development phases and during FMS contracting.

Initiative	Dates
a. Execute one test case with each MILDEP for a new model of customer involvement in the Pre-LOR, case development, and contracting processes of the FMS system.	Oct 2014 – Sept 2015

b. Coordinate and publish appropriate policy changes, informed by assessments of the test cases, for establishing a DSCA policy on increased FMS customer visibility and participation in the FMS process.

Oct 2015 – Sept 2016

c. Conduct annual assessments of effectiveness and affordability of a DSCA policy on increased FMS customer visibility and participation in the FMS process for each of the first two years of implementation.

Oct 2016 – Nov 2018

Objective 6.4: Identify and communicate realistic transportation options and costs before and during case development to improve transparency and responsiveness while ensuring that transportation is resourced at sustainable levels.

Initiative	Dates
a. Develop criteria and execute test cases for advance transportation planning, culminating in the publication of a transportation planning decision tree in the Security Assistance Management Manual (SAMM).	Oct 2014 – Dec 2016
b. Coordinate and formalize processes across the community to identify and consider transportation options before and during case development while ensuring that transportation charges are sustainable.	Oct 2015 – Sept 2018
c. Develop a method for measuring the effectiveness of advanced transportation planning, and conduct regular assessments.	Oct 2016 – Sept 2017

ENSURING EFFECTIVENESS AND EFFICIENCY

7. Applying Resources to Incentivize Community Performance, Innovation, and Responsiveness

Goal: Allocate DSCA-controlled resources consistently and equitably while incentivizing innovation and responsiveness.

End State: A responsive Security Cooperation community is effectively resourced to manage and execute its programs while continually seeking to innovate and improve performance.

Objective 7.1: Define the cost components of the FMS Administrative Surcharge funds budget and formulate strategies that maximize community responsiveness.

Initiative	Dates
a. Establish corporate workload measures to inform the allocation of the FMS Administrative budget.	Oct 2014 – Sept 2015
b. Assess, from a resource management perspective, the cost of Pre-LOR activities and define the portions of these activities that are appropriately funded by the FMS Administrative Surcharge.	Oct 2014 – Aug 2016
c. Assess, from a resource management perspective, appropriate funding sources for continued support of nonstandard program offices.	Oct 2014 – Aug 2016
d. Maximize effective and efficient overseas operations by issuing revised policies and procedures.	Oct 2015 – Sept 2016

Objective 7.2: Transition to a new resource paradigm that incentivizes performance and innovation.

Initiative	Dates
a. Achieve full Financial Improvement and Audit Readiness (FIAR) compliance for all DoD managed funds	Oct 2014 – Sept 2017
b. Establish more accurate and transparent transportation cost methodologies to ensure that transportation is charged and billed equitably.	Oct 2015 – Mar 2016
c. Develop a plan to improve the transparency and accountability of the FMS Trust Fund and other security assistance funds; maximize standardization and best practices; and incentivize improvements and innovation.	Oct 2017 – Sept 2018

8. Optimizing the Management and Execution of DSCA Programs

Goal: Ensure that DSCA leads in optimizing the management and execution of its programs.

End State: The Security Cooperation community, in consultation with relevant customers, continuously improves and optimizes dynamic and innovative processes with appropriate tradeoffs between quality, speed, cost, and transparency.

Objective 8.1: Maintain work quality while more efficiently and quickly processing LORs and LOAs.

Initiative	Dates
a. Publish revised guidance to reduce the average number of days from LOR receipt to LOA/Amendment Offer from FY2013 levels while maintaining document quality.	Oct 2014 – March 2015
b. Annually update a coordination matrix that minimizes the number of DSCA HQ reviews required and facilitates DSCA's quick review of LOAs.	Oct 2014 – Sept 2020
c. Update case writing/review roles and responsibilities for the Case Writing Division (CWD) and implementing agencies to achieve a sustainable workload distribution model that ensures the appropriate level of review and the efficient use of resources.	Oct 2014 – Sept 2016
d. Work with OUSD(C) and OUSD(AT&L) to reduce or eliminate the coordination requirements for nonrecurring cost (NC) waivers beyond DSCA.	Oct 2014 – Sept 2020
e. Review quality assurance and coordination requirements and develop recommendations for future procedures.	Jan 2015 – June 2015

Objective 8.2: Increase efficiency and responsiveness in case execution by codifying the responsibilities of Case Managers and establishing community-wide milestones.

Initiative	Dates
a. Rewrite the Case Managers' responsibilities in the SAMM, C2T.1, making them clearer and more specific so that Case Managers can be more productive.	Oct 2014 – June 2015
b. Establish clearer training and certification for all Case Managers.	Oct 2015 – Sept 2016
c. Standardize key milestones in the execution of FMS projects and make them more visible to the SCC; update the definition of the FMS Master Plan in the SAMM.	Oct 2017 – Sept 2018

Objective 8.3: Establish a standard process to assess DSCA's effectiveness and efficiency in managing and executing its programs.

Initiative	Dates
a. Review existing assessment processes for DSCA-managed programs and develop a plan for a sustained DSCA assessment effort that supports those processes.	Oct 2014 – Apr 2015
b. Where existing models are insufficient or cannot be implemented, develop program-specific assessment frameworks, consistent with monitoring and evaluation principles identified in JP 3-22 and other DoD guidance.	Jan 2015 – June 2015

ACRONYMS:

AECA	Arms Export Control Act
CWD	Case Writing Division
DoD	Department of Defense
DSCA	Defense Security Cooperation Agency
FIAR	Financial Improvement and Audit Readiness
FMS	Foreign Military Sales
G-TSCMIS	Global Theater Security Cooperation Management Information System
LOA	Letter of Offer and Acceptance
LOR	Letter of Request
MASL	Military Articles & Service List
MILDEP	Military Department
NC	Nonrecurring Cost
SAMM	Security Assistance Management Manual
SCE	Security Cooperation Enterprise
SCC	Security Cooperation Community
USG	U.S. Government